D1118878

THE UNIVERSE
NASA

ABDO
Publishing Company

A Buddy Book **by Marcia Zappa**

Buddy BOOKS
The Universe

VISIT US AT
www.abdopublishing.com

Published by ABDO Publishing Company, 8000 West 78th Street, Edina, Minnesota 55439.

Copyright © 2011 by Abdo Consulting Group, Inc. International copyrights reserved in all countries. No part of this book may be reproduced in any form without written permission from the publisher. Buddy Books™ is a trademark and logo of ABDO Publishing Company.

Printed in the United States of America, North Mankato, Minnesota.
102010
012011

 PRINTED ON RECYCLED PAPER

Coordinating Series Editor: Rochelle Baltzer
Contributing Editors: Megan M. Gunderson, BreAnn Rumsch, Sarah Tieck
Graphic Design: Maria Hosley
Cover Photograph: *NASA*: Jim Grossmann April 10, 2009.
Interior Photographs/Illustrations: *AP Photo*: AP Photo (p. 16), Official White House Photo (p. 9); *iStockphoto*: iStockphoto.com/Lya_Cattel (p. 23); *NASA*: Jim Grossmann (p. 19), HQ-GRIN (p. 19), KSC (pp. 17, 29), MSFC (pp. 15, 28), NASA (pp. 11, 13, 15, 20, 21, 25, 30), Pat Rawlings, SAIC (p. 27), U.S. Air Force photo/Master Sgt. Kevin J. Gruenwald (p. 24); *Photo Researchers, Inc.*: Novosti (p. 7); *Shutterstock*: Samot (p. 5).

Library of Congress Cataloging-in-Publication Data

Zappa, Marcia, 1985-
  NASA / Marcia Zappa.
    p. cm. -- (The universe)
  ISBN 978-1-61714-690-9
  1. Astronautics--United States--Juvenile literature. 2. United States. National Aeronautics and Space Administration--Juvenile literature. I. Title.
  TL793.Z293 2011
  629.40973--dc22
                              2010034217

Table Of Contents

What Is NASA?

For thousands of years, people studied space from the ground. In the 1950s, that changed. People began sending spacecraft into space to **explore**.

In the United States, a government group directs these efforts. It is called the National Aeronautics and Space Administration (NASA).

One famous NASA site is the John F. Kennedy Space Center in Florida. There, workers plan and operate NASA spacecraft launches.

5

The Space Race

Many countries wanted to reach space first. The United States and the Soviet Union tried very hard to be first. This became known as the space race.

In 1957, the Soviet Union **launched** the first spacecraft into space. The United States worked hard to match and pass their success.

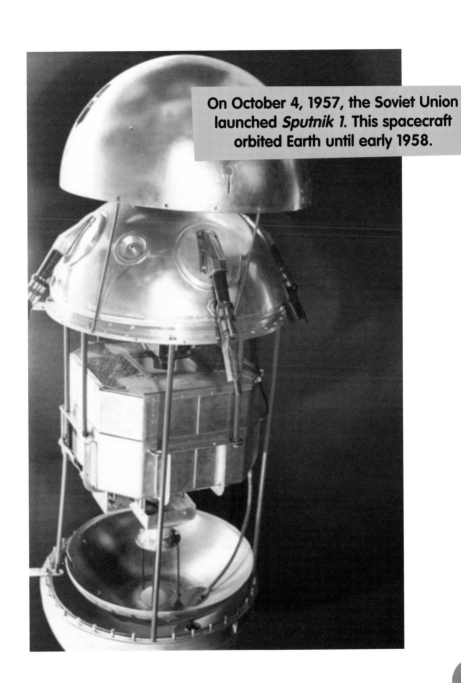

On October 4, 1957, the Soviet Union launched *Sputnik 1*. This spacecraft orbited Earth until early 1958.

Establishing NASA

U.S. president Dwight D. Eisenhower formed NASA on October 1, 1958. It replaced the National Advisory Committee for Aeronautics. This group had studied aircraft flight for more than 40 years.

President Dwight D. Eisenhower

NASA brought many space and flight groups together. Many historians believe this was key to the success of U.S. space **exploration**. Today, the country is still a leader in this area.

NASA astronauts have special training to travel in space.

On Earth, NASA workers track space travel. They make sure trips go as planned.

Early Missions

The United States reached space soon after the Soviet Union. On January 31, 1958, *Explorer 1* became the first U.S. spacecraft sent into space.

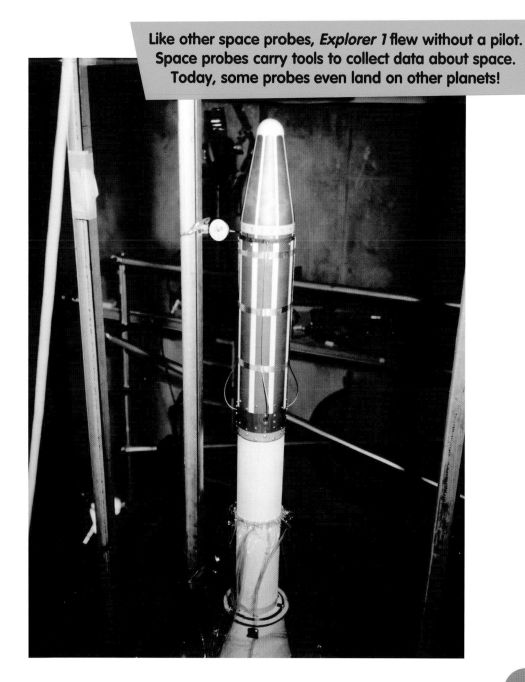

Like other space probes, *Explorer 1* flew without a pilot. Space probes carry tools to collect data about space. Today, some probes even land on other planets!

Soon, NASA began working to send a person into space! But, the Soviet Union beat them to it again. On April 12, 1961, **astronaut** Yuri Gagarin became the first person in space.

One month later, NASA proved it could also do this. On May 5, Alan Shepard became the first American in space.

Alan Shepard (*left*) flew in the *Freedom 7* space capsule (*below*). Powerful rocket engines launched it into space. The flight lasted just 15 minutes!

To the Moon

In 1961, U.S. president John F. Kennedy set a **goal**. He wanted NASA to put a man on the moon. **Missions** to the moon were called Project Apollo.

President John F. Kennedy

Neil Armstrong and Buzz Aldrin flew in the *Apollo 11* space capsule. They landed on the moon on July 20, 1969. They spent 21 hours on its surface.

In 1968, an Apollo space capsule **orbited** the moon ten times. The next year, Neil Armstrong and Buzz Aldrin became the first people to walk on the moon! This was important for the United States.

A New Ship

By the late 1970s, the space race faded. The United States and the Soviet Union had different space **goals**.

NASA scientists began planning a reusable spacecraft. They called it a space shuttle. It would allow **astronauts** to travel to space more regularly. In 1981, NASA **launched** the first space shuttle, *Columbia*.

Space capsules return to Earth by crash-landing in the ocean. Astronauts have to be rescued after landing.

Space shuttles have wings. So, they land like airplanes.

Living in Space

As space travel became more common, NASA began to build space stations. **Astronauts** can live and work in space stations for long periods of time.

NASA's first space station was **launched** in 1973. It was called Skylab.

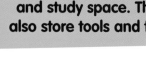
Space stations orbit Earth. They are used to observe and study space. They also store tools and fuel.

In 1998, NASA teamed up with other countries to build a large space station. It is called the International Space Station (ISS).

Three **astronauts** moved into the station in 2000. Today, the ISS has six crew members at a time.

Each crew lives at the ISS for about 100 to 200 days.

NASA Today

NASA has thousands of workers. Its main office is in Washington, D.C. But, work is done in airfields and labs around the country.

Washington, D.C., is the capital of the United States. NASA is one of many important government offices there.

Important Work

NASA scientists work to improve air travel. They create new aircraft that are safer and less wasteful. This is useful for **exploring** space and traveling around Earth.

NASA's work has improved jets and other common aircraft.

NASA also invents new tools for **exploring** space. These tools include probes, spacecraft, and robots!

NASA scientists created humanlike robots called Robonauts. They work with astronauts in space.

Other NASA scientists study our solar system and space beyond. They share what they learn through print, television, and the Internet.

NASA also works to further human space flight. It wants to send humans farther into space than ever before. And, it wants to send them there for longer periods of time.

Today, one of NASA's main goals is to send humans to Mars.

Fact Trek

More than 500 million people watched the first moon landing on television. Neil Armstrong became famous for saying, "That's one small step for man, one giant leap for mankind."

NASA space probes have visited the most faraway planets in our solar system. *Voyager 2* has flown past Jupiter, Saturn, Uranus, and Neptune.

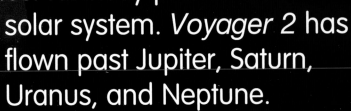

Neptune is about 30 times farther away from the sun than Earth is.

28

NASA mostly works to **explore** space. But, it also uses space probes to study Earth's weather. And, it **launches** communications satellites. These send Internet, radio, telephone, and television messages.

In 1962, NASA launched *Telstar 1*. It was the first communications satellite built by a private company.

Voyage to Tomorrow

NASA continues to **explore** space. It sends probes to test places that **astronauts** could someday visit. And, it hopes to create a new engine for **launching** spacecraft.

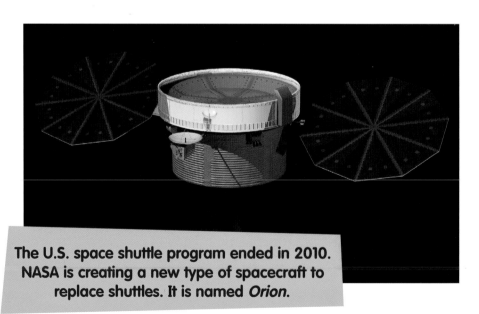

The U.S. space shuttle program ended in 2010. NASA is creating a new type of spacecraft to replace shuttles. It is named *Orion*.

Important Words

astronaut a person who is trained for space travel.

explore to go into in order to make a discovery or to have an
adventure. Exploration is the act of exploring.

goal something that a person works to reach or complete.

launch to send off with force.

mission the sending of spacecraft to do certain jobs.

orbit to follow a path around a space object.

Web Sites

To learn more about **NASA**, visit ABDO Publishing Company
online. Web sites about **NASA** are featured on our Book
Links page. These links are routinely monitored and updated
to provide the most current information available.

www.abdopublishing.com

INDEX